moshi monsters™

SUNBIRD

Published by Ladybird Books Ltd 2011
A Penguin Company
Penguin Books Ltd, 80 Strand, London, WC2R 0RL, UK
Penguin Group (USA) Inc., 375 Hudson Street, New York 10014, USA
Penguin Books Australia Ltd, Camberwell Road, Camberwell, Victoria 3124,
Australia (A division of Pearson Australia Group Pty Ltd)
Penguin Group (NZ), 67 Apollo Drive, Rosedale, Auckland 0632,
New Zealand (a division of Pearson New Zealand Ltd)
Canada, India, South Africa

Sunbird is a trademark of Ladybird Books Ltd

www.ladybird.com

ISBN: 978-1-40939-071-8
006
Printed in Great Britain by Clays Ltd, St Ives plc

CONTENTS

Furi

Diavlo

Katsuma

Luvli

Poppet

Zommer

Greetings, Monsters!

Thank you all sooooo much for sending in all your tricky true or falses, quirky quiz questions and brain-testing trivia teasers to The Daily Growl! YOU made this Superfan Quiz Book and now YOU can test yourself and find out if you're a true monster mastermind! Plus you can even find out which monster type you're most like!

There were so many questions I had to enlist Tyra's help to trawl through them, even my eyes weren't enough to handle them all! Check out our favourite mind-melters in the colour section and meet the cleverclogs monsters that sent them in.

Those guys really made our brains ache!

Keep count of how many correct answers you get, then check out your scores at the back of the book to see how well you've done!

Keep your eyes at hand . . .

Roary Scrawl

First question posted!

Can you buy food for your monster at Horrods?

Awesomeastrid123

GROSS-ERY STORE

FLUTTERBY FIELD

OPEN

Err, I don't know . . .

Answer: No, you can only buy food in the Gross-ery Store

IN THE BEGINNING...

1. What year did Moshi Monsters first open its doors to everyone?

A. 2004. ☐
B. 2008. ☐
C. 2006. ☐

waterbender26

2. Who sends you a welcome gift when you first join Moshi Monsters?

A. Tyra Fangs ☐
B. Buster Bumblechops ☐
C. Roary Scrawl ☐

Emzie1906

3. Who was the first member of Moshi Monsters?

_____

Chelsea1040

4. What is their monster's name?

A. Fuju ☐
B. Billy ☐
C. Snowcrash ☐

Niceboy606

5. How many colour combinations are there when you adopt your monster?

_____

Sillysinger246

6. Which Moshling chews on your cursor when you sign in to Moshimonsters.com?

_____

jj1100

7. When you first start playing Moshi Monsters, what food appears in your inventory?

_____

Chuu-chii

8. How many Rox do you get for winning monSTAR of the week?

Greanie

Main Street

1. Which of these shops is not on Main Street?

A. The Gross-ery Store ☐
B. The Market Place ☐
C. Bizarre Bazaar ☐

Greanie

2. On Main Street, how many ways into the Secret Tunnels are there?

☐

Cupcakes14144

3. What colour is the bird that flies over Main Street?

☐

Jennete904

SHOPS

4. How many construction roarkers are there at the end of the street?

Pinappleheads

5. How many crates are there outside the Gross-ery Store?

blibbyblabby

6. What is the roarker at the end of Main Street eating?

Mkm25809

Food, Glorious Food!

1. What's the cheapest food at the Gross-ery Store?

   A. Essence of Blue
   B. Slop
   C. Toad Soda

   Raptor9090

2. There are three berries on a Sunshine Berry. **True or false?**

   kittykat52

3. Gingersnap is a food available at the Gross-ery Store. **True or false?**

   Emmaandmaddy4eva

4. What kind of fruit is a Zoot Fruit?

   A. Mango
   B. Banana
   C. Watermelon

   Hannahjessica3

Answers: 1. B, 2. True, 3. False, he's a Moshling, 4. B, 5, 6 Rox, 6. A, 7. Slug Slurp Slushie, 8. False, it's a top hat.

5. How much does a Slime Rickey cost?

lilac612

6. Which of these foods is healthiest for your monster?

A. Green
B. Sludge Fudge
C. Spider Lolly

Marpez

7. Which drink was voted Monstro City's favourite?

Monkeymat77

8. The Fandango Mango is wearing a baseball cap.
True or false?

pinkey2399

My Little Monster

1. Name the six types of monster you can adopt.

Swana

2. Only Moshi Members can change their monster's colour. **True or false?**

kool-kat-gal

3. How many Rox does it cost to change your monster's colour at Colorama?

Astonishedman

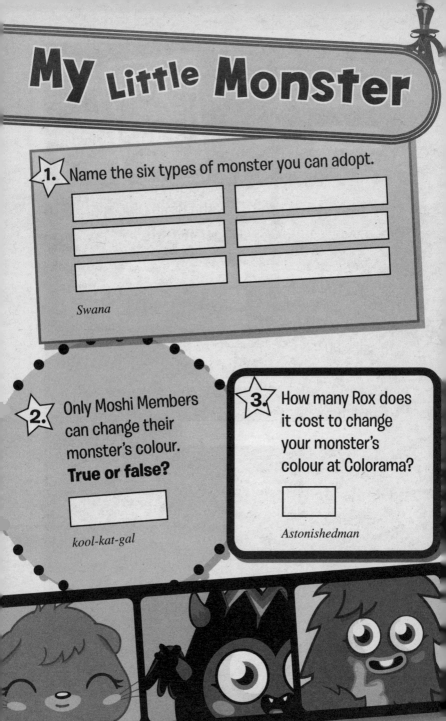

4. In your profile, your monster's health appears above its happiness.

True or false?

shivasti

5. Monster baby photos are only available at the Bizarre Bazaar.

True or false?

fuzzymunchkin123

6. Which monster is missing an eye?

A. Furi
B. Poppet
C. Zommer

Mja2002

7. Diavlo is the only monster that can fly.

True or false?

Newyorkdream787

Answers: 1. Katsuma, Poppet, Zommer, Furi, Diavlo and Luvli, 2. True, 3. 100 Rox, 4. True, 5. True, 6. C, 7. False, Luvli can too.

BREAKING NEWS...

1. Moshi Monsters' News Blog is called *The Daily Growl*.
True or false?

Moshigirlpokemon

2. Roary Scrawl is the editor of a rival news blog, *Newsreek*.
True or false?

nashashas

3. Who is Roary Scrawl's girlfriend?
A. Tamara Tesla
B. Broccoli Spears
C. Tyra Fangs

Tigerskinz

4. Roary Scrawl is holding two eyeballs in his photo on the blog.
True or false?

babybella123abc

5. In his photo, how many eyes are visible on Roary's face?

A. Seven

B. Eleven

C. Fourteen

huntah00

6. What does it say next to the newspaper's name?

A. All the ooze that's fit to print.

B. News, views and ooze.

C. Monstro City's breaking news.

Lilac612

7. What kind of monster guards the entrance to the forums on the blog?

pusscat2

WHERE CAN YOU FIND...?

1. The Googenheim is located at the end of Main St.
True or false?

Matti42980

2. Only Members can go to the lookout in the bottom left corner of the map.
True or false?

xoxoeminemxoxo

3. Which street is nearest to the Puzzle Palace?
A. Sludge Street
B. Main Street
C. Ooh La Lane

Plikky

4. Where in the world is Moshi Monsters created?
A. London, England
B. California, USA
C. Antarctica

Maya2cute

5. Where would you see a
monster with a boom box?

geenahardy1999

6. Which street is the Moshling
Seed Cart on?

angorato

7. Which street does Dr
Strangeglove sometimes lurk on?

dibbin

8. Who rides his bike down
Main Street?
A. Billy Bob Baitman ☐
B. Colonel Catcher ☐
C. Weevil Kneevil ☐

moshimaneb

Answers: 1. False, it is on Ooh La Lane. 2. False, nobody can go there…yet!. 3. A. 4. A. 5. Sludge Street. 6. Main Street. 7. Ooh La Lane. 8. C.

MEMBERS ONLY ...

1. Only members can get Roxy the Secret Moshling. **True or false?**

Cupycakes

2. Where is the only place in Monstro City that Rox trees grow?

maansi806

3. Only members can shop at Horrods. **True or false?**

Junepearl

4. You have to be a Moshi Member to submit your art to the Googenheim Gallery. **True or false?**

Sophiex321

5. What seeds are only available to Moshi Members?

A. Crazy Daisy and Snap Apple

B. Dozy Rose and Silly Lily

C. Mad Marigold and Whistling Thistle

perry9266

6. How many Moshlings can non-members have?

A. One ☐
B. Two ☐
C. Three ☐

Wickiechickie123

8. Only Moshi Members can take one of their Moshlings out for a walk in Monstro City. **True or false?**

RedEyes1w

☐

7. What is the highest number of Rox you can earn by shaking one Rox tree?

A. 100 ☐
B. 50 ☐
C. 150 ☐

Nikkiparkes

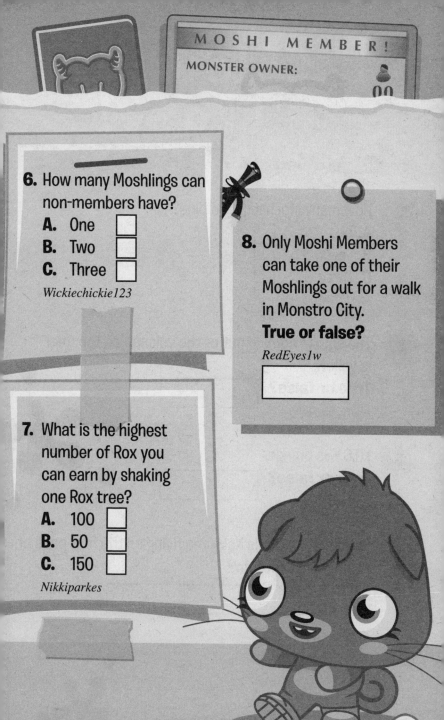

Colour Me Crazy!

1. How many Moshlings are blue?
A. Two
B. Seven
C. Three

ben30774515

2. The smoke coming out of the volcano on the map is yellow.
True or false?

pretty_blossoms

3. I.G.G.Y. is orange.
True or false?

lsprink555

4. What colour kite is Katsuma flying on the first page of Moshimonsters.com?

Rottensatsuma

5. Raarghly, the owner of the Games Starcade, is a small green alien.
True or false?

Ekt333

6. What colour is the Waffle Floor?
A. Green
B. Blue
C. Yellow

Mohit12345

7. Jeeper's stripes are painted on.
True or false?

Zuzser

8. Which six colours of jellybeans appear on the Jellybean Wallpaper?

Lilac612

Answers: 1. A. 2. True. 3. False, I.G.G.Y. is purple. 4. Katsuma's kite is red. 5. False, he is red. 6. C. 7. True. 8. The jellybeans are red, pink, orange, green, yellow and blue.

Sludge Street

1. Ecto lives on Sludge Street.
True or false?

Kaygurl0010

2. There's a couple having a picnic on Sludge Street.
True or false?

gracelynn4

3. What does the fisherman on Sludge Street catch?
A. A fish ☐
B. A sandwich ☐
C. A boot ☐

Lisasawesome99

4. What colour are the cows on Sludge Street?

Mimimimi9

24

5. How many cows are there on Sludge Street?

leafdapples9

6. What is waving out of the window of the vacant building at the end of Sludge Street?

Crabster1999

MOSHLINGS TRUE OR FALSE?

		TRUE	FALSE
1.	There are six Moshlings in each set. *Catjunior*	☐	☐
2.	Buster Bumblechops studies flowers. *Unicorn1213*	☐	☐
3.	There is a penguin Moshling. *Iluvhollister1208*	☐	☐
4.	Waldo is a Tubby Hugushi. *eoin5886*	☐	☐
5.	You can buy Moshlings at the Gross-ery store. *Darkglaceon9405*	☐	☐

TRUE   FALSE

6. Lady Meowford is a fishie.
sophbuddy

7. Stanley the Songful Seahorse comes from Reggae Reef.
erela02

8. I.G.G.Y. stands for I'm Gonna Get You!
nightfury327

9. Members can keep up to six Moshlings in their rooms.
Chainsaw304

10. Beasties can recite the alphabet backwards.
mella84

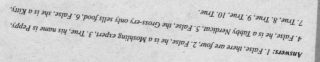

How Many...?

1. How many bats are there on the Bat Mobile?

☐

mybuddyten

2. How many spikes does I.G.G.Y. have?
A. Twelve ☐
B. Three ☐
C. Nine ☐

diamondstar09

3. How many teeth does the My News symbol have?

☐

biancabarb

4. How many food shops are there in Monstro City?
A. One. ☐
B. Two. ☐
C. Three. ☐

wasami

5. How many sprinkles does Oddie have?

☐

fhbratz

6. How many Rox do the Platinum Pants of Power cost?

A. 870 ☐
B. 242 ☐
C. 312 ☐

rob402

7. How many pieces does the Build-A-Bot come in?

☐

Kialn

8. How many Mystery Eggs are there?

☐

bobbythedog

9. How many shops are there in the Marketplace?

A. Six ☐
B. Three ☐
C. Nine ☐

tashasaphi

10. How many kinds of seeds can you buy at the Seed Cart?

☐

elephants98

Answers: 1. Four, 2. A, 3. Four, 4. A, 5. Six, 6. B, 7. Six, 8. Nine, 9. A, 10. Six.

29

LET'S DANCE!

1. In the easy level of the Underground Disco, who is the first singer?

A. Banana Montana ☐
B. Taylor Miffed ☐
C. Hairosniff ☐

netballstar99

2. What is the highest possible score when dancing to one song in the Underground Disco?

☐

Gina83

3. Which Moshi musician wrote Moptop Tweenybop?

A. Zack Binspin ☐
B. Missy Kix ☐
C. The Groanas Brothers ☐

Flabberjack8

4. How many monsters are dancing in the disco?

☐

Qwerty1219

5. What is the name of the drummer in the Fizzbangs?

Rayne2145

6. Complete the names of these Moshling popstars:

A. The [ ] Fighters

B. [ ] Poppets

C. Broccoli [ ]

Robinbirdy6

7. Who sings Peppermizer?

Moonsandpie

8. Who are the judges at the Underground Disco?

Lilac612

Answers: 1. A, 2. Thirty, 3. A, 4. 28, 5. Thwack, 6. The Goo Goo Fighter, Pussycat Poppets and Broccoli Spears, 7. Broccoli Spears, 8. Tyra Fangs, Roary Scrawl and Simon Growl.

HOME SWEET HOME

1. The Cake House style costs 2000 Rox. **True or false?**

Charliebabbage

2. Which house style costs under 1000 Rox?

Blowshi

3. How many Rox does a fourth room cost?

Kizkiz444

4. What appears when you click on the far left tower of a monster's castle house?

Curlycocoa

9. Cap'n Buck has a parrot called Fluffy. **True or false?**

Answer: False, it's called Patch.

8. Which Moshling set is this an anagram for? **RIDE SLOW**

Totororocks2279 👤 14 🇬🇧

Strawberry LEVEL is feeling transcendent

I GOT PRANKED!

530

MY NEW

J LIST

FRIENDS

👤 14

Messages: 530   Friends: 320   RATE THIS ROOM ⭐⭐⭐⭐⭐

7. Which of these is the odd one out?
Cuddly Human, Orange Bowler Ball, Scare-o-plane?

Answer: Scare-o-plane. The others are part of collectible ranges.

6. A. Which Moshling is number 50?
B. What set is it in? **C.** What are the other Moshlings in that set called?

A.

B.

C.

8310bubbles 👤 13 🇺🇸

5. Where was the Orchid in Bloom from Katsuma Clothes freshly plucked from?

Answer: The Fungdoodle Fields.

leopard7   12

Messages: 282   Friends: 473   RATE THIS ROOM

4. What is the name of the statue that sits on a block of cheese?

Lolman11344 13

3. What is the language spoken by Furis?

Joshua
is feeling glum

Messages: 266 · Friends: 84 · RATE THIS ROOM

Answer: Furglish.

2. Cap'n Buck visited the future,
where did he go and when?
A. Futuristic Falls, June 2010
B. Futuretainment Halls, July 2009
C. Jurassic Future, July 2010

Top Trivia

1. Which Moshling do you win by completing the Super Moshi challenge, Missing Moshling Egg?

A. Roxy ☐
B. Big Bad Bill ☐
C. Baby Rox ☐
D. Lady Meowford ☐

Answer: C

One Moshling is not part of each set. Pick the odd one out.

4.

A.   B.   C.   D.

Answer:

5.

A.   B.   C.   D.

Answer:

6.

A.   B.   C.   D.

Answer:

ODD MOSHLINGS OUT

1. A. B. C. D.

Answer:

2. A. B. C. D.

Answer:

3. A. B. C. D.

Answer:

WHICH MOSHLING IS CORRECT?

Some of these Moshlings aren't quite right!
Can you spot the correct Moshling in each group?

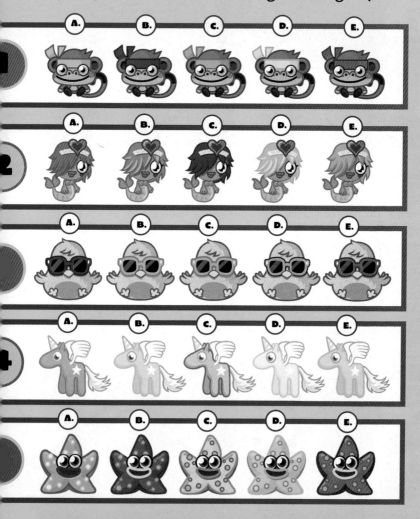

GUESS THE MOSHLING

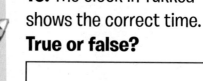

Strakk is feeling transcendent

K LIST

OWNER: 13

Messages: 227 | Friends: 256 | RATE THIS ROOM ☆☆☆

10. The clock in Yukkea shows the correct time.
True or false?

7

8

9

10

11

12

RHIANE3816, SPICEGIRLM2000, GIANNALUVSPANDAS AND MUSIC908.

1 DIY Shop

Can you match these shopkeepers to their shops?

B

2 Dodgy Dealz

3 Horrods

A

4 Babs' Boutique

C

D

Answers: 1.B, 2.D, 3.C, 4.A.

33

Who am I?

1. I am ultra rare, pink and sparkly.
Who am I?

happybunnygirl25

2. I'm purple, fluffy and bouncy.
Who am I?

awesomecarolina

3. I'm white, fashionable and a cat.
Who am I?

Andiza

4. I capture Moshlings with my top hat and cadabra cane.
Who am I?

MrMoshi

Answers: 1. Roxy, 2. I.G.G.Y., 3. Lady Meowford, 4. Dr Strangeglove.

35

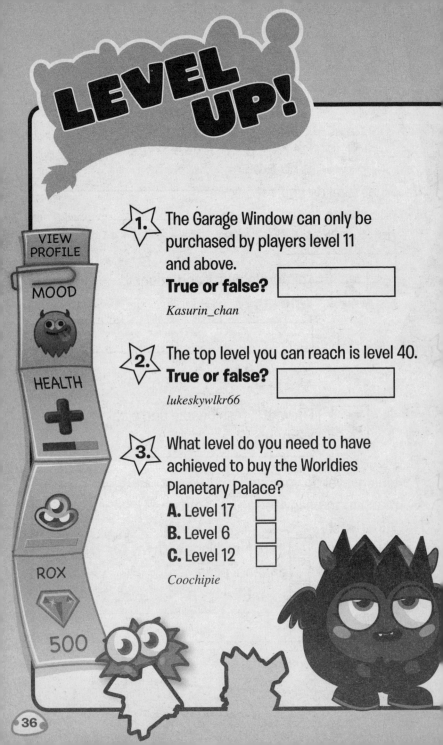

LEVEL UP!

VIEW PROFILE

MOOD

HEALTH

ROX

500

1. The Garage Window can only be purchased by players level 11 and above.
True or false?

Kasurin_chan

2. The top level you can reach is level 40.
True or false?

lukeskywlkr66

3. What level do you need to have achieved to buy the Worldies Planetary Palace?
A. Level 17
B. Level 6
C. Level 12

Coochipie

MONSTAR LEVEL
A
20

4. What level do you need to be to get the Star Clock?

Lilly98528

SCROLL

SCROLL

5. What is the level 16 trophy made from?
A. Peas
B. Rock
C. Teeth

coolcoolc

 6. Which level do you need to have reached to be invited to become a SuperMoshi?
A. Level 3
B. Level 7
C. Level 10

alfiekitten

RATE THIS ROOM

200 VISITS

WHERE CAN I BUY...?

1. The Stormy Wallpaper is only available at Horrods.
True or false?

Wickiechickie123

2. Which of these is not a seed shop?
A. Super Seeds
B. Seed Cart
C. Cluekoo's Plantables

Pizzapaws

3. In the Marketplace, the Zommer's clothes shop is called Zommer's Drop Dead Threads.
True or false?

ninjoe7326

4. The Games Starcade is a members-only shop.
True or false?

mishawbwishi213

5. What is the name of the shop in the Marketplace for Poppets?
A. Poppet's Closet
B. Pretty Poppets
C. Primping Poppets

kitykat1001

Shop Til You Drop!

1. What is the most expensive gift at Gift Island?
  A. You're My Monster of the Week! ☐
  B. Best Friends Forever! ☐
  C. You Rock! ☐

Chantel4

2. Which shop does Snozzle Wobbelson work at?

☐

cutest2009

3. At which shop can you trade items?

☐

Taffy593

4. What sign shows that an item for sale is rare?
  A. A four-leaf clover ☐
  B. A dodo ☐
  C. A gold star ☐

Lulster12

5. What is in a cage in the Bizarre Bazaar?

Missluli5

6. Which of these shops is just for members?

A. DIY Shop

B. Gift Shop

C. Yukea

Junepearl

MOSHLING MAYHEM!

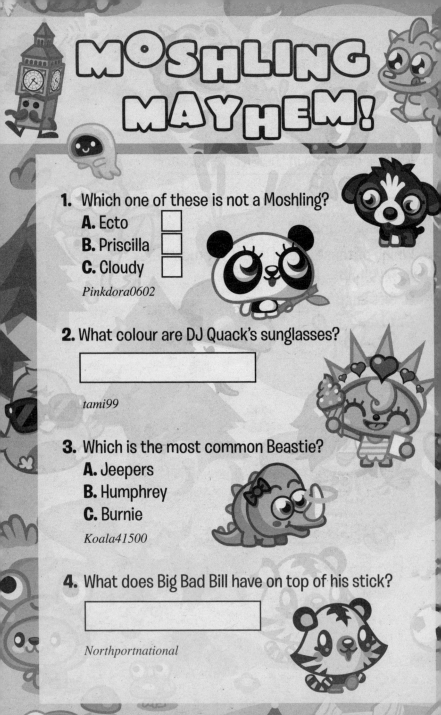

1. Which one of these is not a Moshling?
A. Ecto ☐
B. Priscilla ☐
C. Cloudy ☐

Pinkdora0602

2. What colour are DJ Quack's sunglasses?

tami99

3. Which is the most common Beastie?
A. Jeepers
B. Humphrey
C. Burnie

Koala41500

4. What does Big Bad Bill have on top of his stick?

Northportnational

5. Which of these Moshlings is not a Spooky?

A. Ecto ☐
B. Squidge ☐
C. White Fang ☐

Indigoblue99

6. Which Dino has wings?

A. Snookums ☐
B. Pooky ☐
C. Gurgle ☐

Lovecats1234

7. Which Moshling sings when you click on it?

A. DJ Quack ☐
B. McNulty ☐
C. Cleo ☐

Dogcat30

8. When you log in, which Moshling is sitting on the loading bar with a background of slop?

☐

Pusscat2

JOLLY DAYS AND HOLIDAYS

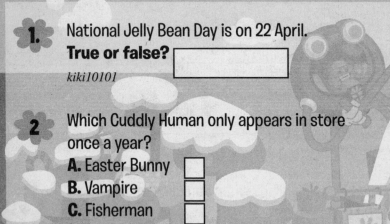

1. National Jelly Bean Day is on 22 April.
True or false?

kiki10101

2 Which Cuddly Human only appears in store once a year?
A. Easter Bunny
B. Vampire
C. Fisherman

Tammi11

3. Roary Scrawl's birthday is 13 February.
True or false?

spengman

4. What do Moshi Monsters call Christmas?

anniethemusicalfan

5. On which day can you buy the Pilgrim's Hat from the Marketplace?

Viprockstar

6. When can you buy Jack O'Lanterns?

Poppetsaresocute9216

7. You can only do the Daily Challenge once a day. **True or false?**

Cuteandfurry12

8 What date is Roy G. Biv day?
A. 13 June
B. 9 April
C. 22 May

baboushka6

MONEY, MONEY, MONEY

1. There are five Rox trees in the Port.
True or false?

Blowshi

2. Each game in the Hall of Puzzles is worth ten Rox.
True or false?

Astonishedman

3. Which game can earn you the most Rox with one play?
A. Flutterby Fields
B. Ice Scream Shop
C. The Daily Challenge

Aydin8615

4. How many Rox do each of the Beanie Blobs sell for?

shivasti

5. What percentage of the original price of an item are you offered at Dodgy Dealz?
A. 40% ☐
B. 100% ☐
C. 50% ☐

gracelynn4

6. How much does a Spicy Dragon Roll cost at the Gross-ery Store?

Agentm1212

On the Map

1. The giant ice cream on Ooh La Lane has four scoops on it.
True or false?

jd45313

2. What is the name of the pirate who docks at the Port?
A. Cap'n Hook
B. Cap'n Buck
C. Cap'n Yuck

Cadbury-monster

3. What colour is the 'choose a location' banner at the bottom of the map?

tashasaphi

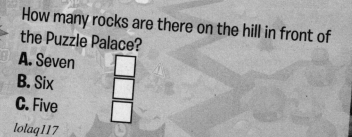

4. How many rocks are there on the hill in front of the Puzzle Palace?
A. Seven ☐
B. Six ☐
C. Five ☐

lolaq117

5. How many candy canes are visible on the map?

☐

memberflower990

6. Where is the Super Moshis' HQ located?

☐

Name?

Moshling Garden

1. Moshlings are attracted to:
A. Food ☐
B. Flowers ☐
C. Your monster's happiness ☐

Sprocket07

2. Which combination attracts Mini Ben?
A. Three black Snap Apples ☐
B. Three red Love Berries ☐
C. Three yellow Crazy Daisies ☐

Blast2001

3. The bird in the Moshling garden is called Mr Sparrow.
True or false? ☐

Loobybx

4. Which of these is a real Moshi plant?
A. Ring Ding Bush ☐
B. Acorn Nutty ☐
C. Love Berry ☐

Boomtater

Answers: 1. B. 2. A. 3. False, it's the Cluekoo. 4. C. 5. Oddie. 6. Coolio. 7. Yellow and pink. 8. Stanley.

5. Which Moshling do you get by growing a purple Star Blossom, a black Star Blossom and a yellow Star Blossom?

Bobbythedog

6. Which Moshling do you get by growing any colour Star Blossom, a black Love Berry and a pink Snap Apple?

Ashleyt6789

7. What colour eyes does the scarecrow in the Moshling garden have?

Keria

8. Which Moshling can you get by growing a Dragon Fruit and two Love Berries?

Thunderfury15

MOSHLING MIND·BENDERS

1. Non-members can't get Big Bad Bill.
True or false?

Softballgurl101

2. What colour is Cleo's bow?

azurial

3. What are Roxy's favourite things?
   A. Vinegar baths and buffing machines
   B. Magpies and fingerprints
   C. Fish and chips

flowers128

4. How many stripes does Jeepers have on each side of his face?

Xxxhoneyxxx12345

52

5. How many Foodies are there?

bluefurred

6. Who was voted the scariest Moshling?
A. Big Bad Bill
B. Squidge
C. Ecto

Snowfrog23

7. What does Scamp want to be?

Ozzyozlem

8. What number does Roxy the Moshling have?

kikicherry456

9. How many known Moshlings have wings?

ay1198

10. How many Moshlings have a bow in their hair?

Chantel4

Answers: 1. False. 2. Purple. 3. A. 4. Three. 5. Four. 6. A. 7. A frog. 8. 101. 9. Eight - Squidge, Angel, DJ Quack, Tiki, Peppy, Prof. Purplex, Gurgle and Burnie. 10. Four – Doris, Purdy, Kissy and Cleo.

TESTING TIDBITS

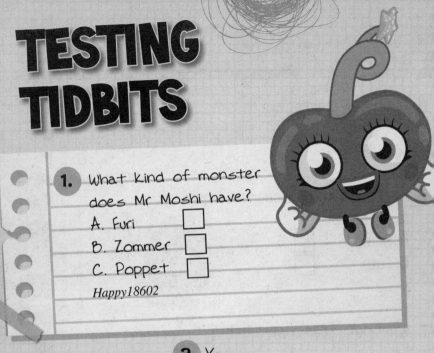

1. What kind of monster does Mr Moshi have?

A. Furi ☐
B. Zommer ☐
C. Poppet ☐

Happy18602

2. Zommer has one human arm.
True or false?

☐

Angeldolly

3. You can send notes to other monsters' pinboards, even if you're not friends.
True or false?

☐

Fozzyweir2001ladybug

4. There is a game called Flag Frenzy in the Puzzle Palace.
True or false?

☐

tinydancer638

5. You can send your friends gifts from Colorama. True or false?

[ ]

Uni_corn

6. When did the Games Starcade open?

A. 2010 [ ]

B. 2009 [ ]

C. 2008 [ ]

coolangel106

7. What is Agony Ant's job?

[ ]

pusscat2

8. What sits in the place of Cap'n Buck's boat when he is away?

[ ]

wowerwebkinz

9. The Pussycat Poppets are orange, pink and blue. True or false?

[ ]

rocol2009

10. How many eyes does the Goggle-Eyed Wall Trout have?

A. One [ ]

B. Two [ ]

C. Three [ ]

Kate21776

Super Moshi Missions!

1. How are you invited to become a Super Moshi?
A. A gift comes to your room ☐
B. A note appears on your pinboard ☐
C. You receive a cape in your chest ☐

mrsmeowkins

2. Who introduces you to the first mission?

☐

rubypinkslippers

3. What does the code say on the arch at the entrance to the Super Moshi HQ?

☐

lsgill79

4. How many stepping stones lead into the base?
A. Three ☐
B. Four ☐
C. Five ☐

idlechild

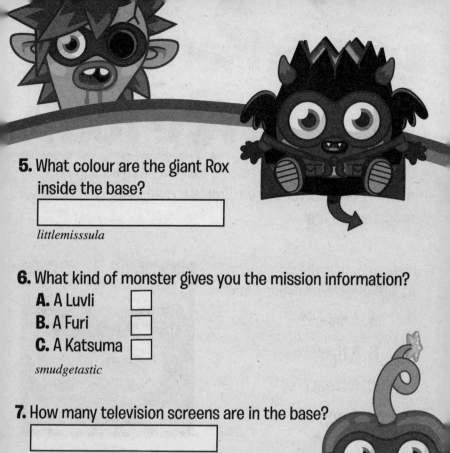

5. What colour are the giant Rox inside the base?

littlemisssula

6. What kind of monster gives you the mission information?
A. A Luvli ☐
B. A Furi ☐
C. A Katsuma ☐

smudgetastic

7. How many television screens are in the base?

pink-tigeress

8. Which of these is the Super Moshi badge?

A.

B.

gina83

Which Monster Are You?

Circle A, B, C, D, E or F to each question, then add up how many of each letter you've circled to see what kind of monster you are!

1. Would you rather have:

A. A snack?

B. A fight?

C. A treat?

D. A bonfire?

E. A cuddle?

F. A new eye?

2. Which kind of music do you prefer?

A. Ballet

B. Techno

C. R 'n' B

D. Disco

E. Swing

F. Rock

3. What's your favourite colour?

A. Brown

B. Orange

C. Cherry red

D. Black and red

E. Pink and more pink

F. Blue and purple

4. What kind of party would you choose?

A. I don't like parties

B. Paintball

C. Dress-up

D. Barbecue

E. Sleepover

F. One with a band

5. Which of these creatures do you prefer?

A. Orang-utan

B. Rabbit

C. Butterfly

D. Dragon

E. Kitten

F. Hedgehog

6. What's your favourite food?

   A. All food

   B. Sushi

   C. Cherries

   D. Anything spicy

   E. Sweets

   F. A bit of everything

7. Which of these skills would you like to learn?

   A. Climbing

   B. Karate

   C. Magic

   D. Fire-eating

   E. Dancing

   F. Playing guitar

8. What kind of things do you like to buy?

   A. Gross-eries

   B. Cool shades

   C. Jewellery

   D. Lava lamps

   E. Cute clothes

   F. New arms

Mostly As - You're a Furi!

All that fur makes you a big softy! You might look glum sometimes, but you secretly love a tickle!

Mostly Cs - You're a Luvli!

You love attention and always like to be the star of the show, but try not to be too bossy to your friends!

Mostly Ds - You're a Diavlo!

When you're angry, you're too hot to handle! But most of the time you're mischievous and lots of fun to be around!

Mostly Bs - You're a Katsuma!

You're always friendly but can be quite scratchy when upset! Decorating your room is one of your favourite things!

Mostly Es - You're a Poppet!

You're sweet natured and adorably cute, but you're definitely no pushover!

Mostly Fs - You're a Zommer!

You're always kind and know that looks don't matter - it's what's on the inside that counts!

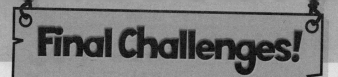

Final Challenges!

1. Which store sells Moshling boxes?

nilly18

2. What is the nearest shop to Babs' Boutique?

horseandpony5

3. Which shopkeeper says "Monsters are my business and business is good."

Swana

4. What does the sign at the Gross-ery Store say?

gracelynn4

5. Banana Montana is the singer of Growliwood. **True or false?**

Thebigfoot1

6. How many Furis can you count in this book?

Chokeymonsters

7. How many times does Dr Strangeglove appear in this book?

HOW WELL DID YOU DO?

Give yourself one point for every question you've got right, then add up your scores to see if you're a superfan or a monstrous loser!

Master of Moshi - over 200

Congratulations on an awesome score! Apply for a job at Moshi HQ immediately!

MonSTAR - 150-200

Well done! With a little more playing you could soon level up!

Almost an Expert - 26-149

That's pretty good going! Keep playing and you could bump up that score a bit more!

Monstrous - Under 25

When was the last time you logged on? Your poor monster must be feeling terrible!